The Search

for

Dry Land

Withstanding the Storms of Life

KATHERINE DYLAN

ISBN 979-8-88540-138-8 (paperback)
ISBN 979-8-88540-139-5 (digital)

Christian Faith Publishing
832 Park Avenue
Meadville, PA 16335
www.christianfaithpublishing.com

Printed in the United States of America

CONTENTS

INTRODUCTION

It is my hope for you, as you pick up this book, that although it is based on a biblical account, you will be able to find hope in its truth. The premise of the book is when you're drowning in the overwhelming waters of life and, no matter what you do, you cannot seem to get solid ground underneath your feet. You keep sinking deeper and deeper with no way out of the flood.

I will bring you some new techniques to challenge you and bring you to a new spot in your life. You will experience some ups and downs and maybe even shed a tear or two, but you will find that through this book, your strength will be renewed. Your confidence will begin to rise, and the solid ground you will stand on will be the firm foundation on which you can begin your next journey.

It is based off the biblical story of Noah's ark, because that is how the story came to me. Whether you are a person of faith or not, you will see the amazing correlations that not only happen in our lives today but also in the lives of Noah and his family. As I was writing this, I used my imagination as to what Noah and his family might have been thinking or feeling in certain scenarios, but the story is straight from the Bible. As a woman of faith, I believe in the accuracy of the Bible and not adding to it. But for the sake of this book, which I believe was God-inspired for you and anyone who reads it, I was merely using this story in the Bible to bring forth the truths that still exist for us today.

I hope this book touches your life in a very powerful way and you can begin to find the dry land that you are searching for!

CHAPTER 1

Giants

There were giants in the earth in those days; and also after that, when the sons of God came unto the daughters of men, and they bore children to them, the same became mighty men which were of old, men of renown.

—Genesis 6:4 KJV

There are giants in your life and mine. They are all around, and we see them every day. You may look around and say, "I don't see any giants." Let's just pretend, for a moment, you are walking down the street and there is a real giant walking down the street in the opposite direction. He is coming right toward you. For a moment, you stand in awe of him and realize you have never seen a giant before. But as his stride is much faster than yours because of his stature, you quickly notice your heart rate is starting to speed up. You can feel the earth tremble with every step he takes. There is a fear rising up inside of you that you can't seem to get control over. You want to run away but find yourself in a very strange and awkward state. There are now voices in your head screaming to run, but there is a part of you who is still thinking you might be friends with him. He is big; in fact, he is gigantic. Your feet are not moving at all, but the rumble under them is growing stronger with every step the giant takes. The very thought of him killing you is becoming very real with every moment. You now can see anger in his face. But now you are aware that running would not help you at all. A new need, to stand and fight this giant, is the only way out.

Still think this story is far-fetched? Let's take a different perspective of these so-called giants. Have you ever stood in that crippling fear just described in the picture above? It is the fear that creeps in out of nowhere—the kind of fear that makes you lose yourself, your purpose, and your identity, the fear that takes over and that you have no idea is even there. You just know you are existing, not able to move at all, stuck in the darkness and pain you feel from the giant in your life that has gotten you here. Chances are, if you are reading this book, you know exactly what fear this is for you.

Now picture that same giant story with another giant or two or three. The fear is the same fear you felt with one, but it is so intensified that you realize life could be over. There is no way out. Sometimes, life will be filled with those giants. It's going to keep you locked in fear for eternity, unless you start naming those giants.

Give your giants names. Don't be afraid to talk to them. Once you call them by name and talk with them, they slowly start to have less power over you. You may even find they have a purpose for your life. They become your allies. It is okay to have the giants come and go in your life. Just take notice of them all around you.

Let's take a look at some of these giants a bit closer. We have already named one as fear. Fear has a purpose, and it is there to help you. Without fear, there could be no bravery or courage. The fear in your life, when not called by name, can be crippling. Fear can limit you and keep you from experiencing so many things in life.

How about naming another giant? We are going to name him anxiety, and he has a close brother named worry. Anxiety tends to show up in the body, and worry lives in the mind. Fear, anxiety, and worry all like to stay close at hand. When paired with each other, they all intensify one another. All three occupy space in your mind and limit your power to transform and become new. It keeps you feeling stuck in the moment with nowhere to turn. The sooner these giants are named and spoken to, the sooner the power resides more strongly in you to take control of your thoughts and mind. The power that has always been inside you and yearns to come out has an opportunity to come forth!

Then there could be a health giant. He could use different names as well. Obesity, diabetes, high blood pressure or heart disease, cancer, pain, or fatigue might be your giant. When these powerful giants are introduced to you, they can be very overwhelming. The diagnosis that may come from a medical doctor may seemingly have no answer that feels good at the moment. However, these giants need to be named as well in order to get crystal clear clarity on how to manage them. When you are stuck in that overwhelmed state of diagnosis and despair, naming your giant will bring you to an acceptance and help you find answers that normally would not have been there.

Let's not forget those stress giants. Financial stress, job loss, divorce or relationship stress, a world pandemic, or even death might be a giant you are dealing with. The stress giants are the ones who come at you at the worst time in your life. These are the ones that, when life seems as about as bleak as it can be, come on strong and could come in multiples. These are things in life that can't be controlled and throw such major curveballs at you. These giants can take over your life in a heartbeat and make you quiver without reason or explanation. Name these giants and allow them space in your life. They have come with a purpose that you need to see and receive from them.

Let's not neglect the friendly giants to name as well. When you are walking through that sea of overwhelm, who are your allies? Who are the giants in your life that will come alongside you and be your biggest cheerleader? Who are the ones in your life that would always be there for you and support you to the end of time? These giants are your support team. These are the thunderous giants of all time. These giants are the ones you will need in your corner when the fight gets really hard and you are ready to sink or swim. These giants will be your life support as the floods come and wash over you and you are barely staying afloat. It's in these moments the waves are crashing all around you and you are so thankful that they helped you build your ark. Your friends, your family, and your allies help you to the new land that awaits you.

With names on your giants, I would like you to play another game with me. I would like you to think of something you used to like to do, but it doesn't seem important anymore. Paint an image of this thing in your mind. Really connect to the senses with this image. Is this image close or far away? Is it in the room with you, or is it outside? Is it big or small, black-and-white or color, a movie or a still picture? Great, now hold on to this image in your mind.

Now take one of these giants in your life, and paint a picture of them in your mind. Ask yourself the same questions to connect your sensory input. Thank you, and now keep this image in your mind as well. Compare them and notice how they are different. If the location is different for the two pictures, we are going to switch them around a bit in your mind. Take the differences from the second image and move them to the first image. So if the giant seems close in the image and the first image you painted is farther away, move the giant to the further-away location with the thing that doesn't seem as important to you now.

You are moving that giant to a different location in your mind, and it will make the giant seem unimportant because the image that you hold is unimportant. This is a very powerful exercise to make the giants seem smaller and manageable. You can approach them because they have names, but they are also in a different location in your mind. Stepping back will allow space in your mind for these giants to just be present but not be so gigantic.

Have you ever looked at a faraway landscape? Sometimes it is hard to spot a bird in the scenery or a tree from afar. You are creating a space for these giants to remain in your life but from a far-off place. The giants seem much smaller when placed so far away. They are the same exact giants, but they hold less power in your life. You are now the giants of your own life—powerful and strong, capable and true. Giants from this perspective will take on a whole new outlook and be the reason your passion, purpose, and identity return to you in that glorious way. Giants will be the stepping stone when the floods recede and the land appears around you. The promise that you will overcome the floods of life and find a new path to clearly walk on will open up for you in an amazing way.

These giants are real. They exist in everyone's lives. Remember they all serve a purpose and how you deal with them will look different for everyone. But naming them and moving them is the first step to recognizing them before the flood hits—creating a space for them to move further away from you, walk through the flood with you, and become your stones of the new life awaiting you. Yes, your giants are real. And, yes, they seem overwhelming, but they are given to you to help you find your power.

I imagine this is what God was seeing as he looked at his creation. The giants were big, mighty men and women. They had the ability to take over the world individual by individual. The only way to save his creation was to bring about a flood, an overwhelming flood that brought about a lot of death in a barren land that had seen no rain, land that was so dry the waters rising washed out everything. The barren lives we lead will get so overwhelmed that when the flood hits it will pour! Will you be ready to bring the right giants on board with you, or will the giants have so much power over you that you will sink with them in the flood of overwhelm?

CHAPTER 2

The Ark

*And God said unto Noah, The end of all flesh has
come before me; for the earth is filled with violence
through them; and behold, I will destroy them with
the earth. Make thee an ark of gopher wood.*

—Genesis 6:13–14a KJV

The giants have been named. It was very possible that when
Noah got the command to build the ark, no rain had ever fallen
before. So this man began building this great humongous boat and
tried to convince people to listen to him when he said rain was coming to destroy the earth. Can you imagine the ridicule that Noah
withstood? I imagine the giants were sitting around laughing at Noah
and his family as he got to work on this big boat—this boat that was
going to save him and his family from an all-powerful God who was
about to destroy the earth. Cackling, thunderous laughing, and bil-
lows of teasing and jekylling could be heard.

The townspeople were also curious. Noah was on a mission!
He and his family knew rain was coming and they had to be obe-
dient. There would need to be so many materials to build this ark.
The trees would need to be cut down, planed, and sanded. The
modern ways we know to do these things were not available back
then, so we have no idea the amount of effort it took to get the

timber ready for the build. God sent very specific directions to Noah regarding the wood to use. He was instructed to use "gopher wood," and although that does not translate to any type of tree we know today, we do know it was a hardwood built to withstand rot and decay. It was a durable material that didn't warp easily and was resistant to fungus.

Then there were the details of measurement. The ark was to be three hundred cubits long and fifty cubits wide and thirty cubits tall. How long was a cubit? It was said that a cubit measured from the elbow of a man to the fingertip. Did you just look at your arm to get a visual? Good, glad to see we think alike. Each piece had a specific measurement to make it work exactly as God had instructed him. The massive height alone to this ark was so incredible when you think they did not have the modern technology as we know it.

Even though the townspeople and giants might have been mocking him, if they were offered the right price, it might have been possible that they might have helped build the ark. There is no record of how many people actually worked on the ark. But we do know it took a few years for it to be built. A boat this size would have had a lot of spectators and even helpers, even if they didn't believe the rain was coming.

But one thing we do know is God was very specific about the height, depth, and width of the ark. He gave Noah very detailed instructions on how to build his ark. God knew the needs of Noah, his family, and the animals even before he gave the instructions to Noah. He was breathing life into Noah and his family in ways that Noah didn't even know about. He just had to trust. It made no sense and was a trust Noah just had to step into without an understanding of why or how. It was faith in action.

Based on the last chapter, we all have giants in our lives. They are there for a purpose. Giants come into our lives to give us more depth to our journey. And let's pretend now that the ark is symbolic of our intuition, that feeling in our gut when we can't explain what is happening and we just know it is, the very thing that people do not understand and the thing that when tapped into will never lead us wrong. The depth of it can withstand any inclement weather and help us navigate the waters of life. It also has a purpose, and it can save your life from drowning in the sea of overwhelm.

When you listen closely, God whispers into your heart center where your intuition lies, and he gives you specific details to follow to build your ark—the measurements, the type of wood to use, every little detail on how to make it perfect for you. Be open to the way these insights come in for you. They could present as energy or a still small voice. It may be a prompting or a rumble in your spirit. It could be in the form of dreams or visions. Sometimes even shapes that form behind your eyelids can give way for the knowledge to come in. I encourage you to find your way to find that voice for you.

There may be people in your life who do not understand what it is that you're doing, just like Noah. But by listening to your heart center, you are able to make decisions for yourself that will protect you and keep you safe when the giants come at you. You have a new method of safety and belonging. You get clear on the information that is coming to you and are able to powerfully step into the truths of who you are. You also have a trick now to keep your giants further away.

How do you listen to that intuition? I would like to suggest finding a meditation or two to listen to in order to tap into that amazing potential. Now meditation may seem like something that goes against your beliefs. I used to think that too until I realized that when we pray, we are speaking to God. When we meditate, God speaks to us. By adding meditation to your life, it will quiet the other voices in your mind that cause doubt and clatter, the voices that scream to you in the night like the sound of a siren or a screeching bird, the voices that keep you feeling frozen, motionless, and unable to breathe. Silencing these voices gives you power and strengthens that intuitive muscle and finds that there is creativity there waiting to be expressed. Will God lead you to build a big ship? Probably not, but you will be able to sense the inner spirit leading you to new places and opportunities.

There is no shame around not understanding if the voice you are hearing is in fact your intuition. It is a skill and a muscle that needs to be strengthened. Your own voice can speak loudly, and it can become very confusing if it's overanalyzed. Let your inner voice become the louder voice. It may not make sense, and that is okay. Just be quiet and allow space for turning up the dial of that voice. It's in the silence that the soul speaks.

I also suggest getting in the habit of journaling. The insight you receive in the meditations can be very productive, so writing what you discover in these moments can be very useful. There is what they call the twilight hours between 2:00 a.m. and 5:00 a.m. where inspiration hits. Taking the time to journal your insights will help you gain clarity in your life. The moments when you first wake up are very powerful moments. Listen in the time when your subconscious mind is active and allow those heightened intuitive moments to occur.

Another powerful way to tap into your intuition is to exercise—a simple walk around the neighborhood or yoga or stretching. These are all ways that your body can speak to you. Are you allowing your body's voice to become present with your decisions or allowing it to speak to your soul? By getting more in tune to your body, the soul's voice will become deeper. Try different things to see what it is that your body wants more of. Be okay with movement in any form.

Connect with nature. Get outside and listen to the birds chirp or the melody that comes from the animals and the wind, the raindrops as they softly hit the rooftops, or the way the soothing creek sounds as it bubbles over the rocky terrain. Let the grass tickle your toes or the sand wash over your feet. Feel the emotion of the clouds and the heat of the sun on your brow. Look at the amazing way God kisses you each morning with the spectacular colors of the sunrise. Glance at the magnificent beauty that surrounds you in the evening with the sunsets. Feel the cool air with the fresh fallen snow or enjoy the way God speaks through the crevices in the snow piles that shine blue with his love. Wrap your arms around the gardens of growth and transformation. Celebrate the seasons that come and go, and with that change be okay with the things that come up for you. Step into that place of peace and learn to embrace the majesty that unfolds around you every day.

Being in a constant state of prayer and gratitude can also heighten your intuitive powers. There is nothing wrong with experimenting with what works for you. If what you are doing points you more in the direction of God's love, then go in that direction. Feel the energy that arises in you. Find your passion and tap into it often. It not only will strengthen your intuition but will feed your soul in a natural loving way. It will make you come alive in ways you never knew could be possible.

Build your ark with the specific directions God leads you to. Put away the cackling and teasing that may ensue because you listened to the heart of God for you. Silence the giants that may not understand the rain is coming. Get yourself ready to withstand the worst flood of your life and any other that may come your way each and every day. Step into your ark, step into your faith, and close the door to those who don't want to listen to your own voice of wisdom. There will always be those who do not understand, but knowing your own personal truth will allow you to withstand the storm.

CHAPTER 3

Pitch

Make thee an ark of gopher wood; rooms shalt thou make in the ark, and shalt pitch it within and without with pitch.

—Genesis 6:14 KJV

God told Noah to line the entire inside and outside of the ark with pitch. Now *pitch* here is defined as "a sticky resinous black or dark-brown substance that is semi-liquid when hot, hard when cold." It is made out of coal tar in today's age, but in Noah's time, it was probably made from the resin or sap from the trees. It not only made a waterproof layer on the ark but also protected it from decay and rot.[1]

God told Noah to make rooms and line the inside and outside with pitch. Pitch is a covering that would protect the ark from any pests. And it provided a dry place on the inside of the ark for the beds for the animals and Noah and his family. It also was able to keep the food safe from moisture and mold.

I recently took a trip to Kentucky to visit the Ark Encounter. It is hard to imagine the size of this boat until you walk upon a similar model. It was built as a replica of the ark Noah had built, based on

---

[1] lexico.com

the sizes mentioned in the Bible. But lining the entire inside and out with a very sticky substance in order to waterproof it seems like a big accomplishment to me. Sometimes, it seems rather hard to just make a peanut butter and jelly sandwich without getting sticky jelly everywhere. But to coat the entire boat, both inside and out, with pitch seems really tough. But it was for their protection.

Another reason for the waterproofing on the inside of the boat was also suggested at the Ark Encounter. Noah and his family would have needed to collect rainwater so they had a good source of drinking water for both them and the animals. Also, they suggested that there might have been a moon pool inside the ark that purified the air. The crashing waves would pull in the fresh air and push out the animal smells as the waves went out.

I would like to take the opportunity to help you learn to calm yourself in the face of a storm. There are many ways available, but I would like to focus here on the moon pool technique. The moon pool would force air out that was bad and pull in air that was good. When the storms of life are hitting you and you feel your heart racing, you can calm yourself down by controlling your breathing. Take a deep breath in through the nose to the count of five. Go at a pace that is comfortable to you. When you have reached five, hold it for five. Then release the air for a count of seven. Again, in through the nose for five, hold for five, and out for seven. Keep doing this a few times until you have gotten into a nice rhythm. Then on the next inhale, imagine inhaling the clean air of joy and peace, and hold it. Then on the exhale, breathe out all the stress and worries that are coming at you. Continue to purify your airspace with this breathing until you feel like the raging storms of your life have calmed down a bit.

We know the practical reason for the pitch. The ark had to be weatherproof to withstand the rain and flood that were coming. But again, let's relate the pitch to God's anointing or atonement. God has laid a covering over all of us as protection if we believe in him. He becomes our protection, our barrier, our shelter, and our atonement. Just like a parent would protect their child from running into the road and from any sort of danger, God also protects us in the same way.

Atonement can also be viewed as a cluster of ideas to cleanse the impurities. If God asked Noah to line the ark with pitch, it was also to cleanse any impurities from the ark. There are many ways to cleanse yourself of impurities today. I invite you to explore them with me for a moment. This is not an exclusive list of things to do, but a good guide into things that you can do to start to purify your life. It only requires small movement in the right direction to see an immediate impact.

The first thing I would encourage to cleanse your body of impurities is to limit consumption of addicting substances. Things like alcohol, nicotine, caffeine, and sugar all have a huge impact on your life when consuming too much. By keeping these things in your life in abundance, you actually invite anxiety and sickness into your life. Mental illness is a promising event by inviting addictive substances in large quantities.

Get good-quality sleep. Good sleep raises serotonin and allows the natural happiness to emerge victoriously. Getting good sleep may require a new mattress or investing in some pillows and setting a scene of tranquility in your bedroom. Shutting down electronics and having a quiet hour before bed is also another very great way to improve your sleep patterns. Begin to form a routine and set sleep hours for yourself. Eliminating caffeine and alcohol, which are diuretics, can also help because you are not needing to run to the bathroom in the middle of the night. Use natural daylight to your advantage. Natural daylight increases your melatonin production, making sleep more natural at night. Also, watch your food consumption before bed. Some foods can aggravate your digestive system and make your sleep uncomfortable.

Change your diet to less processed and more natural ingredients. Replacing your junk foods with a fruit or vegetable can begin to change the pH of your body. Your body will naturally cleanse itself from the inside out when the pH of your body gets more into a natural state. So how do you start making these changes when you have no idea where to start? A good rule of thumb is to shop the perimeter of your grocery store. When you shop into the middle, they introduce so many processed foods, like cereal and snacks. If you do go into the center of the grocery store, limit what you buy.

Moving your body more in fun ways can also cleanse your body of natural toxins. This can be anything that truly speaks to your soul. Once you tap into the intuition that you have built with your ark, movement can become a way of life. Movement can flow from inside of you, and your body will want more. Find what feels right for you. Enjoy how it feels in your body. Let your soul speak what it wants to do. You will find exercise is so much more enjoyable when you allow it to come from within. Do what you love to do and set an intention for showing up for yourself in a whole new way.

By covering the ark in pitch, both inside and out, it kept the judgment waters outside. We all have giants that come to destroy us, we all have our ark of intuition, and now we have the atonement (or cleansing) of pitch to keep us protected. There is nothing that the giants can do to us that is not going to be protected.

That doesn't mean we won't have the giants or things in life that could destroy us. There were many times in my life that as I reflect back on them, I realize God protected me from the harm that surrounded me. I have had abuse, which I have survived. I was driven to bankruptcy by a marriage that completely drained me of my identity. I have been curled up on the bathroom floor in tears, thinking my life was going to end at any moment. My faith has been shaken in so many ways, but God walked with me through it all. There were times that I didn't sense God around me, but he was always present with me. By tapping into our intuition and relying on God's pitch or covering over our lives, we have the tools and the means to withstand the giants and floods and even be transported to a new land that is amazing.

CHAPTER 4

Clean and Unclean Animals

Of every clean beast thou shalt take to thee by sevens,
the male and his female: and of beasts that are
not clean by two, the male and his female.

—Genesis 7:2 KJV

God brought the animals two by two to the ark, but he made sure there were more clean animals on the ark than unclean. Why were there more clean animals than unclean? The clean were needed for food and also for sacrifices on the new land. God wanted to preserve the animals on the earth. But he also needed the animals to preserve Noah and his family while on the ark and the new land he would repopulate.

Now with this knowledge, let's look again at what we have discovered so far. The giants were on the earth, and Noah was told to build an ark and line it inside and outside with pitch. He brought more clean animals on the ark than unclean. In our lives, the giants are real, our intuition will guide us, and God's covering or pitch will protect us. But what do the clean and unclean animals represent in our lives?

I am going to say they represent our thoughts. Our thoughts can keep us stuck in life. Or they can become the very thing that lets our feet get firmly planted on dry land. What thoughts are going on inside your head right now? As I sit on the beach writing this, I ponder the vastness of the universe. I am enthralled with the oceanic wildlife that I am seeing. But wait. I need to get my dishes washed. The kids need to be picked up from school. What day is today? I have that thing coming up on the nineteenth. Look at the amazing clouds today. What if I were to start something new, like biking? I could never bike very far as a kid. Dumb idea. Wow, looks like a storm is coming. Good thing I am building this ark.

Have you ever noticed how easy it is to completely lose yourself in your thoughts? How about when you are considering something new? Do you hear the negative voices on replay in your mind? Those unclean animals take up residence in the cages of your mind, ready to attack like a ravenous wolf or a mountain lion ready to pounce. The thoughts in those cages are ferocious and untamed, ready to prey on the weakest minds. By keeping the unclean animals on board your ship, the waves will inevitably continue to toss your spirit to and fro. The vomit that will ensue from the seasickness of the messed-up life you are building will not only stink up your ark but rot it as well. Your ark will sink, and you will go down with it—no hope of dry ground to stand on, no lifeboat, no hope of the beautiful new land that is waiting once the floodwater recedes.

The clean animals are there for food and nourishment and ready to leave the ark to rebuild that life that is coming with every rainbow you see. When the rains stop, and they will, you will have tamed the wild animals of your mind. The thoughts you think can be those that give life and feed and nourish your soul. Those are the animals you want to keep around when your feet hit dry land. Those are the animals you want to reproduce in that new stunning life you're building. In what ways can you manifest more of those clean animals? Let them take up residency inside your mind. Feed them, care for them, and treat them well. You will see the animals are easily tamed, but you need to nourish them. When they start to form, let them be the animals that repopulate the amazing life you want for yourself. Let these animals be the ones to withstand the storm.

Therefore, by keeping more negative thoughts inside our hearts and minds (unclean animals), we could end up with more of the same negative thoughts and outcomes—not a place I would want to be in when the winds start to howl and the rain starts pouring down. We need to stand firmly on solid ground by replacing them with positive thoughts (clean animals) that we would like to see manifest more in our new land of life where we will be sprinkling the garden of growth and transformation.

There is a reason God wanted Noah to eat the clean animals. It would keep him healthy and give him more energy. By that analogy, when we feed ourselves with positive thoughts and intentions, we keep ourselves healthy and full of energy. Tap into that newfound energy. We have already found so many ways to begin to prepare our hearts for the floods of life. By nourishing our hearts and souls with this positive energy, we will start to manifest those positive things in our lives that would need to be there to help us live an abundant life when we come out of the flood.

When trying to change your energy levels, you tap into those positive things that are there already. The more you have, the more you can reproduce. The same thing happened to Noah. There were more clean things on the earth to manifest more good things on the dry land. It would be a great way to repopulate the new land.

Survival would have been destroyed if it were the other way around. When too many negative thoughts populate your being, your survival is at stake as well. It is harder to tap into your intuition, and it feels as though God was nowhere to be found. You begin to manifest more problems and seemingly push God further away. Just like that, it begins to rain like you've never seen before. It not only rains; it pours.

CHAPTER 5

The Flood

*And the waters prevailed exceedingly upon
the earth; and all the high hills, that were
under the heaven, were covered.*

—Genesis 7:19 KJV

We've all heard the saying "When it rains, it pours." Imagine the giants and the townspeople as the rain started to fall. Never having seen rain before, they were probably very curious as to what was happening. I presume it was pretty dry there, so the water might have absorbed into the earth at first. They might have been thinking, *This isn't too bad. It feels kind of refreshing. Noah could have stayed out and enjoyed it, too, and not built such a big boat.*

Then the rain continued, and the ground was saturated. Waters started rushing all around. They probably started to get a little fearful. When the rain hit their ankles and even their waists, things were starting to get real. They probably started swimming and scrambling to find higher ground. When the waters eventually got high enough, they started to drown. Noah and his family were safe inside God's protection.

The waters on the earth filled the earth. Water came down from the sky and also up from the earth. The ark was picked up and carried by all the rushing waters. The area I live in Upstate New York has five rivers that flow through it. When it rains hard, we inevitably see some flooding. However, our area has also seen two major floods in the past fifteen years, both of them happening within five years of each other. So as a bystander watching the floods happen, I can give firsthand experience to the feelings and emotions that go along with back-to-back flooding.

During the first flood, I lived on a hillside that had a steplike appearance. When the rain started, I couldn't see the effects of it at first. I was kind of closed off to it and didn't even know it was happening. When the public broadcasting system made an announcement across the television and radio stations telling people to get to higher ground and seek shelter, I began to take notice. I had a grocery store at the end of my street and decided I better get some extra food. I went to my car and headed down the road. Much to my surprise, the bottom street was already flooding, and so was the grocery store. You see, even though I was not feeling the effects of the flood myself, I was able to see the effects coming all around us. Needless to say, I wasn't able to get the groceries I needed, but I was still provided for. I had a dry home and really plenty of food to make ends meet for a few days. But others during this time were not so fortunate. When the rain stopped and it was safe to do so, we drove around the area to assess the damage.

Trees were down, houses were under water, some had even been moved to a new location, people were living in shelters, and dirt and debris were everywhere. Power was out for most, schools were closed, and the rescuers were still on the search for missing people and pets. Just absolute devastation everywhere. Once the water went down, people got to work rebuilding their lives. New homes were being built. Cleanup to the streets and land was happening all over. People were pitching in wherever possible to help each other. Still my house was untouched and not needing any work at all. We all recovered and felt relief.

Skip ahead five years, where a lot of people had just finished their recovery and newly remodeled homes. I had moved this time to a place near a creek, in a low valley, in our area. I had only been there for about a year and a half. We were in our own renovations due to just purchasing the home. Guess what. It started to rain again.

This time it was raining harder, and I could see it happening all around us. The street was being evacuated at both ends but not at our house or the neighbors' houses yet. I was watching the backyard and neighbors' yards very closely. It started out seemingly simple. Things were floating by in the back field. It started out as simple as a ball, then a television, and then a refrigerator. Things progressively got bigger. Eventually, my kids and I noticed a house floating down behind our house. We recognized it as the house that sat on the corner, not even a quarter of a mile away from us. I ran to the front of the house to get a better view of what was happening. Water was bouncing down the road and coming straight for our house. The neighbors' houses were just about in the flood. Only by an act of God did the water flow down our driveway and turn the opposite direction and go behind the neighbor's house.

There were a total of five houses in our area that did not get evacuated, and we were one of them. So imagine the fear as I did, as we watched the waters rising all around us and the devastation of the land. There were people who had just rebuilt their entire homes from the previous flood that were completely under water again. How could this supposed one-hundred-year flood be hitting us all again in five years? Nobody could imagine it happening all over again.

To feel the fear in the moment of the flood was unreal. Can I now bring you to another personal story of mine? I managed to live through two major floods with actual rain, but floods of life were hitting me hard. Sometimes in life, things start to get real. The giants in my life were coming at me from all sides. When the rains came, it began flooding me with all sorts of emotions. You might have felt at some time in your life you were drowning and there was no way out. I know, because I have been there too.

I had been through an abusive marriage, where I had very much feared my life and kids' lives at the end. I managed to get out and get a new home. I had many health issues happen at the same time. I was getting tested for almost everything at that time, trying to figure out what was happening to me. Was it multiple sclerosis, a stroke, or just nerve damage? Nobody seemed to have any answers. It was then I was diagnosed with PTSD from the effects of the marriage. It pulled me out of work as a pharmacist and left me with no income for a while. The fear of losing my new home became so very real, and month to month I would just barely make it. I knew I couldn't work as a pharmacist anymore because it would trigger the PTSD so badly. In the meantime, I was also battling the grief of my marriage ending and my career ending, and life as I knew it was over. With the divorce pending and a ton of marital debt I was stuck with, there was no way out but to declare bankruptcy. The floods of my life just kept coming down. I felt like the rain kept falling. I was at rock bottom, sinking deeper and deeper. Where was God? Where was my lifeboat?

The sinking devastation that came over me created this stuck feeling. I knew I had reached an ultimate low and was in the middle of a world with no way out. Would I answer the call or let the struggles get the best of me? My determination needed to be stronger than my devastation. I pondered this thought for a while and needed to be sure of where my heart was leading me. I could remain in this dark storm of life, or I could choose to change my life for the better and begin a healing journey that would be so powerful even I would not recognize myself in the end.

Then I became determined to not let this be my end. I had a whole new story that needed to be written. I was in search of dry land—a whole new beginning to my life. I was being hit with a storm, tossed and turned by the waves. Every direction was pelting me, and I had nowhere to go. So I hear this story of Noah and his family on this ark and am fully aware of the process on the boat. The giants were real, the ark had been built and the pitch lined the inside and out, the animals both clean and unclean came, and the waters were all around. God was still there and had me on his ark, away from the giants I had known my entire life and covered with his pitch on the inside and out! I was ready to answer the call on my life and withstand the storm.

CHAPTER 6

The Waiting

*And after the end of the hundred and fifty days the waters
were abated. And the ark rested in the seventh month,
upon the mountains of Ararat. And the waters decreased
continually until the tenth month: in the tenth month, on the
first day of the month, the tops of the mountains seen.*

—Genesis 8:3b–5 KJV

Now Noah and his family had been on the ark for a very long time after the initial forty days and forty nights of rain. When we are in a waiting season of our lives, it can feel like an eternity. You know the rains have stopped, but you still aren't quite finding the dry land out there. You know it exists, you can vision it very clearly, but the search goes on. What do you do?

It's in this season the best things happen, and don't get so caught up in the want or desire to miss the season you are in. Let's take a look at those giants again. They are in the past, but you still remember them. There was fear, anxiety, financial woes, grief... You fill in the blank for your giant. They were real, but you no longer see them. Sure, you may get triggered from time to time, but how did you get here?

In my searching and waiting period, I became a health and life coach. The schooling occupied a lot of my time, but the biggest transformation happened in that time. By taking up a practice of meditation and journaling and being coached myself from the various coaches I had met in school, I started to transform into the person God made me to be. Now everyone's season of waiting is going to look different, so be curious as to what the waiting means to you.

I had just come out of an abusive marriage where I thought my life was going to end, I had PTSD, and I had lost my job as a pharmacist. My debt was huge from the marriage, and there was no end in sight. Bankruptcy was hanging over my shoulders. I had to decide whom I wanted to be through all this. I started creating some healthy boundaries that enabled me to survive this wait. There was a lot of healing that needed to be done, and it was time to get unstuck and really embrace the vision I had waiting for me.

My journey on my ark, surrounded by water, started with a simple revelation. I needed to find my worth and value. I was raised in church, and even though I knew God loved me and he made me in his image, I still had a hard time stepping into that truth. You see, my giants had become so mighty that, that was all I could see. Sometimes it's not that our giants are so big; it's sometimes we feel so small. With the giants now under water, they were still very real for me. Then the transformation in me began. I was at the lowest point imaginable and really had a choice to make: either I go under with the water or I climb up and wait for the mountaintop experience.

When I realized the first truth—that abusers seek qualities in others that they do not possess themselves—I started to realize all the qualities I brought to the table. I was strong, I was a survivor, I did what I could do to protect my kids at all costs, I was a good mom, I was the best wife I could be given the situation, and I was a leader. I was capable. I was learning a new truth about me. I was actually confident. I was learning to love myself and honor myself and my decisions. It was gonna be all right. The worst was over. So I started to climb the mountain.

Then I realized the second powerful truth, which was that I was valuable—not just in God's sight but in the realm of our world. I was created in God's image, and he doesn't make mistakes. He says a good woman is more valuable than rubies. My value was there the whole time, but I never saw it in myself; and suddenly I felt my confidence rising. I had stepped into some powerful truths about myself, and all of a sudden, I knew I wasn't going to go under and sink. I took another step to the top of the mountain. Are there some powerful truths you need to accept in your journey to take the first steps to the mountaintop?

Before long, I was also experiencing more energy because my confidence level was also climbing. I was feeling unstoppable. I had momentum moving, and it felt great. It started with two steps forward in the right direction.

I decided to begin a daily meditation and journaling some insights into what I was feeling. It required me to be fully present with the waiting period I was in, not to think of my past or live in dreamland all the time. It required enjoying the moments of present time and releasing the worries of tomorrow. Being so present allowed me to become aware of all the things around me, tools so to speak, which God gives to us as resources. Things in my life became so vivid, in color, vibrant, and alive for me. Even the biggest woes during this time became blessings. Waiting is never easy to do, but the blessings that surrounded me were everywhere. I just had to stay present with the here and now to see them.

I also at this time began to get specific about what my new world was going to look like. I held a very strong vision for my future land I would get to step out of the ark on. The vision was so crystal clear because I had tapped into my intuition (my ark) and I was there with no place to go because the waters were still on the earth.

This was the next big step for me, and I encourage you to step into some new truths about yourself and then let a future version of you emerge. Start to let yourself dream about any potential thing that you would like to see happen. Let go of any doubt that it can happen, let go of any expectation on how it will look, let go of the negative self-talk, and just enjoy the fact you get to dream. Whatever the journey to get there is, know there are no mistakes. Write any insights you may have at this point down. Don't worry if they seem completely far-fetched and unbelievable.

A big piece of building this dream for me was to let God take over the dreams. I started to just step back and let God take the wheel. I threw any timetable out the window because I had no idea how long the waters would be on the earth. I started to tap into listening to what God was inspiring me to do. I tapped into the intuition that he gave me, and it made my connection with him so much stronger. When I went to church, I was no longer afraid of what people thought of me. I was able to raise my hands, cry, and sing out loud, without a care in the world. I was stepping into another powerful truth about me. As I said before, I was raised in church, and I had never experienced what I was experiencing every time at church and throughout the week. It was so powerful. The closer I started trying to get to God, the closer I actually became. He was always there waiting for me, but I connected in a real way this time. Things in life, the giants, that I used to fear started to become smaller and smaller. I was becoming more powerful, and the power that the giants used to hold started to fade.

There are still times the giants come out, but I have learned to observe them. I gracefully accept their presence to become more curious as to why I am triggered by them. But I look at them from an observer, instead of the one being in front of them. By stepping back to the observer mode, I am able to recognize them for who they are and the message they're trying to tell me. Then I address the message, not the giant. When you do this, the giants go away again. They are no longer serving their purpose, and I remain walking with God on my ark. The blissful state that remains in me allows me to tap into God's leading ever more.

Now Noah, I presume, was going through his own waiting experience. He still had his everyday tasks to attend to, like feeding the animals and cleaning up the rooms. But he had this incredibly long waiting period. It may not seem that long to us when you look at the actual time of close to a year, but imagine seeing rain for the first time and really having no idea when it would be safe to leave the ark. He was probably thinking if the food would last. He would have to give that over in faith to God. He was probably thinking if he could in fact repopulate the earth with just his family. He would have to give it over to God. He probably dreamed of the new land that he would step out on. But he would have to give it over to God.

Release the outcome, release the control, and find your freedom. I received a massage on the beach this morning and realized a few things about control. When we are always up in our control of things, it builds up tension and stored energy that has no place to go. Learn to relax into trust and understand you may not have the exact path of how to make your vision become the dry land you walk on. The storms that come your way will toss you to and fro, but with every crashing wave you get closer to your destination. When I let go of the control on the beach, the massage therapist was able to move my muscles in a way that brought healing and a release of the tension in my sore muscles. Some of the muscles I didn't even realize were sore. If I didn't let go of that control, the knot in my muscle could continue to get worse and eventually cause medical problems. This is a knot I didn't even know was there until she pressed on it.

The season of my healing was one of the toughest ones of my life. The only way through it was to give it over to God. But in the waiting time for my new land, I let God take control of the outcomes. I saw the vision ahead of me and had no idea when it would come to pass. But amazingly enough, when I stepped out of the way, God was able to do abundantly more and in a faster time period than if I tried to steer the ark alone. And it didn't always come to pass the way I envisioned it, but the land he was preparing for me was out there, and it was beautiful! He just had to work out the details!

CHAPTER 7

The Raven

And it came to pass at the end of forty days, that Noah
opened the window of the ark which he had made:
and he sent forth a raven, which went forth to and fro,
until the waters were dried up from off the earth.

—Genesis 8:6–7 KJV

Many times people can hear the story of Noah and his ark and not hear the part about the raven. When I reread this story before writing my book, the raven stood out to me. I had been raised in church and had heard the story of Noah's ark many times before and had never realized a raven was sent out first. It made me stop to think about the significance of that particular bird and why it was so overlooked in the story.

The raven, in the Bible, was considered an unclean bird. At the time of Noah, there were certain animals that were considered acceptable for sacrifices. Did you ever stop to ask why if they were unclean were they on the ark anyway? The unclean animals at the time were still okay to eat because there weren't laws about the eating of the unclean in place yet. I imagine Noah and his family fed off the animals and also fed the other animals to keep themselves alive on their journey.

Why then did Noah let a raven go first off the ark? A raven is also a bird that is a scavenger-type bird. It would have been able to leave the ark and feed off any dead carcass still lingering in the water. It would make sense that it would not return to the ark and Noah would still not know if the floodwaters had receded. The raven would have been able to fly around and eat whatever it found and would have no reason to return to Noah for its security. I like to think it was a way to purge the ark of the negative stuff that Noah and his family had gone through in the search for dry land. Noah would've known the bird was not going to come back and that he was also sending it out into the world again to clean up anything dead still on the outside that could contaminate the new world he was going to rebirth.

If we picture the ravens in the ark story as things that we need to get rid of in our lives, this paints a beautiful picture of the importance of the raven. I struggled quite a bit with the writing of this chapter. You see, I have walked this journey, just as you are now. I was in a very dark place and needed to be healed in many ways. The pain and trauma are now behind me, and I am in a very blissful state. When I experience emotion that is out of line with the natural peace and joy that came with my healing, I find myself not wanting to go back. So I avoided this chapter like the plague.

When I discovered that the emotional state of joy and peace was not conducive to writing this chapter, I chose to stay happy and blissful. The chapter kept calling out to me to write, but in order to do so I had to let myself feel these emotions that I hadn't felt in a while, and it honestly scared me to see what I might uncover. Perhaps it was another giant trying to make its way back into my life. When it came down to it, I knew that I was about to experience another part of my healing journey, and I knew I would be better off for it in the end. However, it is never easy to uncover dead things that have been buried for a long while.

Eventually, I got to work on the chapter and had to uncover things in my life that I had buried. What did that look like for me? A lot of soul-searching to see what this chapter meant for me and really what the chapter might look like for all the readers. The first thing that began popping up for me was material stuff. What kind of stuff was in my life that I no longer used? I found the place I felt led to begin was my clothes. I took a day and purged my closet and drawers of things I had been holding onto for those "what ifs" in life. I was shocked to see me fill three bags so easily of stuff that I hadn't worn in quite some time. I still had plenty in the end. I found a new freedom that I hadn't experienced in a while.

That was just the beginning. As I write this chapter, there is still much of my house I will be purging, getting rid of the unused stuff in my life that I buried and haven't used in a while. But it got me thinking, *What else may be dead in my life, or what is something else that may be causing me death in my life that I could get rid of?* My next thought went to the food I consume and how, if it is not healthy for my body, it is time to let it go. I am a sweet food eater, and I also have diabetes. Although I know sweets are not good for my body or diabetes, there is a sense of security in eating them. I can somewhat control my sugar by the medications I take, so why take that next step into giving up the junk food? Well, because. Because I am on this journey to find dry land just as you are and a part of that journey for me is getting rid of the junk in my life that no longer serves me in a way that takes me to where I am going. My health is important to me, and I do not want to live on medication for the rest of my life. I do not want to end up with kidney problems that run in my family or neuropathy or blindness from diabetes. The thought of a healthy life resonates with me so much more now. So out with the old!

The next thought I had was, *How do the places I go line up with what my future self is wanting or desiring? Are there places in my life that I need to let go of and not go anymore because they are holding me back?* Check in and see. Then let them go. *What about the job I do? Is it in line with where I am going?* This one is a tough one. Again I find security in this paycheck that my job provides for me. But I have realized it is not in alignment with my current focus on life and it's time to let it go—maybe not today but very close in the future. But I can see it doesn't align with where I am going, and it feels so draining to go in day after day. It is a toxic environment and doesn't make me feel good anytime I go there. By letting the raven go from my job, I can step into where my passion is. I know it needs to go soon, and I can also start preparing the way for when it's time. This is something to keep in your mind as you are letting go of things. Some things you can just let go of, but others you may need to prepare for before releasing them.

My thoughts went onto any other areas of life that I may have dead stuff lingering. You see, letting a raven go is needed quite a lot as you start to grow. It may need to be let go from some deep hurts from your past. I realized for myself that there are patterns I have developed over the many years of my life that I needed to unbury. In order to bring the doves out and experience peace, I needed to dig a little deeper. What I uncovered one time was I had been holding on to behaviors that I needed to let go of so the vicious cycle would stop repeating itself.

I uncovered that there was a part of me that ever since I was a little girl would allow things to happen to me that were not very positive things. It required me to dig a little deeper to discover it, but it was something that no longer was lining up with who I am today. I learned in this time period of letting go and writing this chapter that I needed to speak up for myself more. You see, as a child when these negative things would happen, I responded in the way a little girl with my knowledge could respond. But those behaviors were never okay for me, but I didn't know how to tell someone the behaviors were wrong. I didn't know how to tell them to stop, and I didn't know how to stand up for myself. So when one person did something to me and I allowed it and didn't speak up, it solidified that behavior in my mind. The behavior was negative, and the way I responded was the best I could do with the knowledge I knew. But because I survived the incident, I was training myself to not speak up the next time or the next. For me, letting go of this thing in my life has brought so much freedom. Just because I survived the incident over and over again does not make the incident right for me or anyone. It just set me up for manifesting the same behaviors over and over again.

Maybe you may be feeling a lot of what I am saying resonates with you on a very deep level. Take a peek at your life and go all the way back to your youth. Are there any patterns of behavior you find repeating over and over again? Maybe, like me, you dealt with it at an age-appropriate knowledge of how to help it. But now that you are older, if you want to get rid of these repeating behaviors, you have to use different knowledge to reprogram your brain. It may not line up with your new pattern of behavior and your core values anymore. It's okay to reevaluate from time to time to reprogram your brain to catch up to where you are today. It is okay to retrain your brain to respond in a way that sets healthy boundaries and allows your voice to be heard. No judgments, no expectations, and just realignment. Then once you do, do not be afraid to let your raven fly away from the ark. Let it soar to new heights, cleaning up the dead stuff that no longer serves you!

Ravens in the Bible were also used in other stories as a provider. Sometimes it can be scary to let things go. But just as a raven is symbolic for getting rid of the unclean on the ark, the raven can also be symbolic for the provider. In order for new good stuff to come into your life to feed off, you need to let the raven go to get rid of dead space. By getting rid of the old dead stuff, God will send new blessings into your life in ways that you never knew you needed. It may not happen overnight, or in the way you think it will, but it will show up in an abundance of blessings. Be open to the next step after letting go, of letting in, letting in that beautiful peace that comes with it all!

CHAPTER 8

The Dove

Also he sent forth a dove from him, to see if the waters were abated from off the face of the ground; but the dove found no rest for the sole of her foot, and she returned unto him into the ark, for the waters were on the face of the whole earth: then he pulled her in unto him into the ark. And he stayed yet another seven days; and again he sent forth a dove out of the ark; and the dove came in to him in the evening; and, lo, in her mouth was an olive leaf pluckt off: so Noah knew that the waters were abated off the earth.

—Genesis 8:8–11

Can you feel it? The anticipation that Noah had when he let the first dove go must have been huge. He had been cooped up in the ark for quite a while at this point. The rain had stopped, and I presume the sun was shining. Noah could see a vision of the new land he was going to live on. He knew it was going to be so incredible, but he had to send the dove out to see if it was time yet to come out of the ark. I assume there might have been an excitement filling his soul of the good things coming.

But then the dove returned, and there was more waiting to happen before he would be able to see the new land. A lot of times in life you may have experienced this. You may even be experiencing this right now as you have walked with me through this book. I know I am. I have been in this state for a while now, and I realize it's just not time yet to have that new land. God is still working out the details and teaching me patience. So as Noah sent out the second dove, in anticipation, how his heart must have leapt when he saw the olive branch.

The dove returned to him with an olive branch. The branch was green and full of new life. It was a small glimpse for the new land still to come, but the vision was getting clearer every day. The dove represents peace and hope for the new world and for Noah and his family. There was a celebration of sorts on the ark as the new life was seen in a better view. God would save them, and hope filled the air. However, in their hope, they still had to be more patient and wait a bit longer. Noah and his family had to release one more dove to know the time had come. That was the best dove to be released yet because she didn't return.

After you have walked through a storm or flood of your own, you may have landed in a dark place just as I did. It didn't matter which way you tried to step out. The ground beneath gave way. It was landing on the ark of your own life that saved you. You may have even had an awakening on the ark. So your anticipation of what is coming in your life may be getting the best of you too. There is a peace that has surrounded you and filled your soul. You have surrendered. You can see a slight glimpse as to the joys coming your way. It's time to release your first dove.

Send out some feelers to see if the waters have really subsided—or if the rain has stopped at least. Sometimes, when that overwhelmed state hits you and you feel like you are drowning, it is hard to see how deep the waters actually are. Things have been coming into your life that shook you up in a bad way, and now the weather is shifting, and new things are coming at you. These new things are also shaking you up a bit, but you are starting to realize that this is a new fear you have never experienced. It's a fear because you are living outside your normal comfort zone. New opportunities begin to form, and by taking this new fear and experiencing these new opportunities as they come, you begin to be transformed, a transformation that God has equipped you for since you were a child. You also walk with hope because you are feeling so alive. You are now walking in alignment with your soul.

But it's not quite time to leave the ark yet because you need to tackle these newfound fears. As you look inside these new fears, a peace grows within you. You begin to realize that these fears are ones that bring a new sense of being to you. You realize these new fears aren't really fears that slow you down but ones that propel your growth forward. It is in letting go of these fears that healing begins in exponential ways. It's in letting these fears go that they transform from fears into challenges. So let your first dove go, and don't be surprised when it comes back to you. It's not time yet.

Keep working on yourself, keep growing, and keep healing. It may be getting closer to the time when you let that second dove go. When that dove returns with a new branch full of life, the excitement will fill your soul like it is filling mine right now. Oh, that beautiful land that is coming your way seems so amazing! God starts opening up new opportunities and fun synchronicities along the way just to confirm you're growing in just the right ways. He keeps you walking with him and leading you down new paths—each one amazing in itself but each one perfectly timed to deliver you to that new land in his timing. Be patient.

Let go of expectations of what and when that new life is coming. This is really the hardest part of my journey. Every day, I let go of what this new life will look like. You see, I have painted this picture in my mind. And the more I hold on to that picture in my mind, the less likely I am to allow God to do what only God can do. It's by letting go of this picture in my mind I learn to see God's goodness and his divine leading. I am still crystal clear here as to the vision of the new land, but I have let go of the idea that it has to be exactly the way I have pictured it in my mind's eye. Allowing God to paint that picture as he sees fit is a key element here. If you take nothing more away from this book, it's this right here. This is the premise on which this book is written.

When I was just figuring out this concept in my own life, I realized that each and every day is a new opportunity to release my dove. That dove can fly around and come back to me as many times as needed to keep myself free of expectations. Some days the dove flies back to me quickly with nothing in its mouth, but sometimes, I release it and it comes back with that life-filled olive branch. I am able to step into that faith and peace that God is sending me to help me know in my heart I am on the right path.

Letting go of expectations does not let go of the hope or new land that is coming. You can still be in eager anticipation of what is to come and know with hope in your heart that the outcome will appear. It is essentially the law of sowing and reaping. You have planted seeds along your journey, and you can be sure those seeds will produce a harvest, but only in the season it is intended for. So hold on to the hope that your new land is coming. But stay present with the current seeds in your hands. They may need more cultivating.

Along the way, people may come into your life to take you to your next opportunity. By being present with the here and now, you will be able to recognize these helpers when they come. You will use your intuition muscle that you have strengthened in the waiting period on your ark and realize that these people arrived at just the right time. The people who come into my life all start to come into my life for a reason. I don't always have to understand their role in my life, but sometimes their role is so much more obvious than others. I know they have come into my life to bring me peace and happiness and fill my soul with joy in the waiting times. God is not done with the details of how it comes together. So I wait. And sometimes that wait seems so long, and sometimes it can feel like it's right around the corner.

I am able to stand in a solid place still on the ark, knowing in my heart that the best is yet to come. I can be assured that no matter what may seem to be taking place in the real world, nothing is going to rock me like my flood did in my life before. The abuse and trauma are gone. The giants in my life are dead. I have been protected by God's covering and grace and have let go of the many dead things and unclean things in my life. Each time I let out my dove and it returns with a bigger olive branch than before, I know it's almost time to leave the ark. It's time to step out on dry land. So I will release my last dove and step onto the solid ground that God has led me to all along.

CHAPTER 9

Dry Land

*And it came to pass in the six hundredth and first year, in the first
month, the first day of the month, the waters were dried up from off
the earth: and Noah removed the covering of the ark, and looked,
and behold, the face of the ground was dry. And in the second month,
on the seven and twentieth day of the month, the earth was dried.*

—Genesis 8:13–14

That glorious day had arrived when Noah got to step off the ark
for the first time since the flood. The land was dry, and he got
to start walking on solid ground. Oh, can you imagine? How it must
have felt to walk on dry land again. The smell of the earth after a rain
instead of the ark. The sight of the trees and the colors around him.
The sound of silence with no animals in his ears, demanding food
or water or a cleaning. The taste of maybe some fresh fruit growing
already. And, most of all, the feeling of knowing you made it through
the worst storm of your life and could now step on solid ground. Oh,
how his senses must have filled him with deep compassion and gratitude. The Bible says that he made an altar to present to the Lord his
burnt offerings. The sweet smell from the offering pleased the Lord.

The first steps out onto solid ground must have felt amazing.
You and I also have come to a place of walking through the most horrific storm of our lives and can now start the process of rebuilding.

We are ready now, and God has equipped us for this exact moment. The day we can finally stand on solid ground has arrived. The storms are over, and you are stronger than you think. You are more capable of anything you set your intentions on. You are loved. You are amazing.

What is the first thing you will see, do, or feel? Where is it that God has led you to? The ark didn't land in the same location that it started in. There is a reason for that. The new land that you will possess has new life in it. It is not possible to go back to that old life because it no longer exists. There is no turning back, and why would you want to?

The life you lived before is what brought the giants and storm into your life in the first place. You have walked an amazing journey with me to name your giants and stand up to their ridicule. You have covered yourself in God's protection. You have let go of the bad things in your life and replaced them with more of the good things. The floods came, and you were protected. You were safe and on the road to your healing journey. You learned to wait in God's place he had you build and learned so much in that time. You also had many opportunities for healing and for growth. You let out your raven to clean up any lingering thing that might have still been dead in your life, and then you filled yourself with peace and sent out your doves to know when the timing was right. The road you have taken is far from over, but let's not forget the many things you have accomplished so far. Your journey has been amazing. Take some time right now to reflect on your growth and offer up some gratitude for all the things in life that have happened for you (not to you) for this exact moment. Let that sink into your soul. Breathe into that space as we continue.

Have you taken time to appreciate all that you've done? Good. The space you just held in gratitude will now become your anchor. I would like to talk for a moment about something I just touched upon in the previous paragraph. The things you have walked through, as tough as they seemed at the time, were all happening for you. God has allowed those things to come into your life for this exact moment. God has equipped you to live more powerfully now than ever. You have seen heartache, pain, fear, anxiety, depression, and maybe even some trauma or abuse. I will never discount the walk that you have walked through because it was real. I know as well as anyone else. The things I suffered from were horrendous, and never would I want to relive them or have anyone else walk that road. But I can also see that they were given to me to grow me in so many ways.

There were positive intentions around all of them. Yes, even the parts that seem so horrific to put words to all had positive intentions. Take some time to discover them for you. This will take you from a victim to a victor mentality. Stop blaming everything on everyone else and accept full responsibility for all that came your way. This does not mean that what was done in your past was justified, especially the abuse. But by accepting responsibility for it, coming into your life gives you the power to see it from a new perspective. It allows you to have power over it all, no shame or guilt on yourself, and please forgive yourself for those mistakes you made. By blaming others, you remain a victim and are giving power away to the abuser. After all you have gone through, your power belongs to you. When I thought my life was going to end by my ex, I struggled to find a good intention. But now on the other side of it and through all the transformation I have endured, I never would be here writing a book if there wasn't a positive intention for it. I am stepping out on dry land with a whole new perspective on life, and hopefully you are too.

Take a step back from your story for a moment, and watch parts of it on a movie screen in your mind. Can you see yourself going through the details in your mind? Get curious with yourself for a moment and see what the world sees in you. What are your strengths that you hold on to now because of what you walked through? Maybe you didn't feel strong at all. But if you watched a close friend walk through the same stuff and they responded just like you, would you be able to see the positive strength in them? Start to name and write down a few. When you have come up with as many as you can for that one movie of your life, move on to another and another. Pretty soon you will start to see your strengths emerge forth. You will start to see the good intentions behind everything you went through. You will find that a new confidence will arise in you.

With that newfound confidence, take the first step onto solid ground. Step into a new version of you that will become more and more apparent to you with each step you take. Let the new opportunities enter your life and step with confidence into these opportunities. You will start to see that when your focus is on positive things, more positive things come into your life. New doors opening are inevitable for your continued growth. The ground you now walk on is dry, and you have stability with every step. You have started on a new journey.

Take another step onto the dry land. This time let gratitude fill your heart. Notice the new you and how much you have changed from the start of this book. All that was happening for you was allowed to bring you into a new land—one that is so incredibly beautiful that your old life seems like a distant memory. Allow gratitude to overflow from your core because you did survive the greatest flood to ever come your way. You did survive that sea of overwhelm. You did survive the giants. You did survive the worst imaginable stuff. You survived!

Pace yourself, and let the real you begin to emerge. Let the animals leave your sanctuary and begin to rebuild your life with grace and ease. God will show you the next move to make when it's in his timing. Continue to grow as you wait. Plant seeds every day to instill a new life for yourself. Let those seeds be watered and nourished until they flourish. And remember to look at the trees. They are strongly rooted now, and the branches are strong, but the fruit is the last thing to develop. Trust yourself in your new growth, and never give up faith that the seeds you are planting now in the dry ground will turn into an amazing garden to sustain you into your future!

CHAPTER 10

The Rainbow and Promise

I do set my bow in the cloud, and it shall be for a token of a covenant between me and the earth. And it shall come to pass, when I bring a cloud over the earth, that the bow shall be seen in the cloud: and I will remember my covenant, which is between me and you and every living creature of all flesh; and the waters shall no more become a flood to destroy all flesh.

—Genesis 9:13–15 KJV

Noah was replanting and repopulating the earth, and God sent him a rainbow in the sky. His ark had landed on top of a mountainside, and he could see the valleys below. The colors were vibrant in his new land. Then God decided to paint more beauty in the sky. But with this majestic rainbow, God made a promise to Noah. He promised him that never again would the floods destroy the land. What a powerful truth to step into as Noah was rebuilding his life.

This is such a powerful truth for you and me as well. We can rest assured that there will be no floods that come into our lives that will destroy us. We now have new ways of handling them and standing on solid ground. The past is dead and gone, and we have a new life waiting for us. Does that mean we may never have to suffer again? I wish that it were possible for me to tell you that, but I am sure suffering will come and go just as it has in the past, but this time you are armed with the powerful truths of who you are. You are much stronger and more confident. Your feet walk on solid ground. You will be able to withstand the storms of life because you are rooted in faith.

What does this amazing future look like for you? Maybe you haven't had an opportunity to dream about that yet. As a life coach, I am in constant conversation with people, asking them this very question. I get to see the life transformation they are still about to embark on. I get to lead them down that path for a longer journey. I want to invite you along with me on this new journey.

Let's take that very question and explore it a bit deeper now. What does that amazing future look like for you? Let's pretend for a moment that you are walking in one of those valleys that Noah could see from his mountaintop. As you are walking down a path and looking up, you see a hot-air balloon. It begins to make its descent down the valley, and you can tell it's coming down to get you. Without fear, you have a knowing that you are supposed to get in. The pilot of the balloon opens the basket door and helps you in.

As the balloon lifts off the ground, you feel yourself going higher and higher. The rainbow hovering over you in the sky fills you with peace. You can begin to see your life and the broader picture of your life come into view. As the balloon takes you higher and more of this view comes into being, take in the sights and sounds that surround you. Are you able to see the mountaintops yet, or are you still lifting upward? Can you hear the birds chirping and the flame shooting into the chimney? Is there a breeze in the air? What are you feeling? Can you feel anything else on your skin or in your heart as you lift higher and higher? Close your eyes for a second, to embrace these thoughts. Then go ahead and look beneath you now. There is a piece of your life that is in full view now. You can see your future self below. What is it that you are doing? Just take it in without judging it or playing a critic. Let that part of you just watch the scene as it unfolds before your eyes.

Your pilot has a walkie-talkie to the future you, and he hands it over to you in the balloon. What is it you would like to ask this future you? Is it something you may need to learn from them? Is it something that maybe you need to acquire a new skill for? Ask them for direction in how to live your life right now to make that picture you see below become a reality. The future you answers all these questions for you with ease. You look up and see the rainbow again and realize God's promise has been made to you as well. Notice the feeling you are experiencing right now. Enjoy the view from the hot-air balloon, and know that before you go back down, the pilot mentions to you that you are able to come join him on the mountaintop as often as you like. He will gladly bring you to that place so you can see the future you anytime.

You are very grateful. But before you descend, you have one last question to ask through the walkie-talkie. Ask your future self what they would like to be called. Your future you is holding a gift. It is placed on the ground. Then take the time to thank yourself for all the insight you were just given. Slowly the balloon starts to make its descent back down to the new land you are working on rebuilding. With each part of the descent, the broader image becomes narrower and narrower. Finally, you reach the ground, and the pilot opens the basket door to let you out.

Now you spot the gift that was left for you. Go over to it and open it. See what your future self left you. I encourage you to take some time and journal what you saw. Write down the answers to your questions and make sure to write down your future self's name. I encourage you to find your future self and the pilot often. They have a special gift for you each time you see them and get to ask new questions.

I have done this future self exercise quite a few times myself and also with clients. I am amazed every time that my future self has the best gifts. Some of these gifts have had such special meaning, and some have even brought me to tears. It's truly amazing to see the power in this exercise. My future self's name is Hope, and credit goes to her for allowing me to write this book. By visiting her, I have been given many opportunities as an answer to my questions. It is not until later, months later, that they come to fruition. One time even my gift was so profound that I had no idea why the gift came to me, only to find out a few days down the road the true meaning revealed itself. My mind hurt in a good way because I was so baffled that Hope knew the exact gift I would need in a few days' time. So I encourage you to visit your future self often no matter how crazy people may think you are.

It's amazing the things you can learn from your future self. You have received a valuable gift in God's promises and in that rainbow. You can step onto that dry land in confidence and know in faith that the land you are rebuilding is safe from any further destruction. You have found the dry land you were searching for!

CONCLUSION

It is my hope that you have thoroughly enjoyed this book. I also am praying that your journey that you have gone on with me was helpful to you. I am a transformational, clarity, health, and life master coach. I work with people every day stuck in the harsh reality of the world they are living in, with the sea of overwhelm, guilt, shame, and trauma. I help them find their dry land and find the next step to rebuild their lives.

Though these exercises in this book have been tried on countless people with success, I do not claim it will work on everyone. However, if you find that by going through this book something has come up for you that you would like to gain more clarity on, I encourage you to connect with me. I would love to come alongside you to help you through these issues.

Trauma and abuse, anxiety, fears, and worry are not a one-size-fits-all sort of thing. They are different for everyone and stem from many different beliefs and upbringings. I am trained to unpack those beliefs and help you find your true identity, the identity that God has designed you to be. I enjoy working with people as they step into the truth of whom God made them to be. It is my passion to help mediate this change and have people live into their greatest potential.

God is a master crafter and made each of us with unique gifts and talents. When we are not living into them the way God has designed us to, we are not able to serve God in the way he intended. I don't know about you, dear friend, but I do not want to hide my talents under a rock. I want my talents and gifts to be used mightily in a way that God says to me, "Well done, good and faithful servant."

So if you are struggling at all with knowing what your God-given gifts are and don't know how to use them, I encourage you to connect with me. If you are struggling to know your worth and value, connect with me. If you are struggling with who you are and what your purpose is, connect with me. But most of all, if you are struggling with that sea of overwhelm, the floods are hitting you from all around, and you need to find that dry land to stand on, connect with me. I want to help you in the search for dry land. Thank you for taking the time to read this book, and if you found it helpful, please share it with another.

ABOUT THE AUTHOR

Katherine Dylan, author of *The Search for Dry Land*, has grown up in faith since a child. She is the mother of three kids and a grandmother to one. She is passionate about helping others through challenging times and is currently living her purpose of a women's empowerment, transformational, and clarity life coach.

Her life has not always been sunshine and rainbows, because with every rainbow comes a storm. Katherine has walked through many storms of life and now has overcome it all. The circumstances that brought her to her transformation all happened for her to allow the passion in her to form and to be equipped for this exact moment.

With purpose her life story has been written, and now she steps into a place of gratitude and sharing. She has realized that in her sharing, healing happens for not only herself but others as well. Storms hit everyone, but having the right mindset in the face of storms can make all the difference in the world.

Katherine would love to speak at women's events and share her story in whichever way she is invited to do so. She has risen from victim to victor, financial ruin to prosperity, diseases to health, a spiritual disconnect to amazing faith, and low self-worth to a God confidence. Her strong faith propels her forward without fear.

CPSIA information can be obtained
at www.ICGtesting.com
Printed in the USA
BVHW050448161022
649211BV00002BA/96